THE Bunny Make-It Book

Mazes, games, and easy gifts to make for Easter

Designed and illustrated by June Goldsborough

Happy House Books / New York

 Published in the United States by Random House, Inc., New York, and simultaneously in Canada by Random House of Canada Limited, Toronto. ISBN: 0-394-84970-1. Manufactured in the United States of America 1 2 3 4 5 6 7 8 9 0

A-mazing Bunny

Randy Rabbit is lost! Help him find Mommy Rabbit by marking a path through the maze for him. *(For the answer to this and other puzzles, see page 24.)*

Which Two Mice Are Alike?

Only two of these rainy-day mice are exactly alike. Can you find them? *(Answer on page 24)*

Easy Easter Egg Candy

To make these delicious little candies, mix one egg white with one cup of confectioner's sugar in a bowl until you have a stiff paste. (Ask a grownup to help you separate the egg white from the yolk.) Divide the paste into several small bowls and add a few drops of different food coloring to each. Take teaspoonfuls of the sugar paste and mold them into egg shapes with your fingers. Soon you will have a whole plate of little sugar Easter eggs!

Who Has the Most Eggs?

To play this Easter game, first trace the egg shape below onto thin, light paper. Nine or ten paper eggs will be enough. Then color the eggs, cut them out, and put them in a big dish.

Give each player a straw. At the word "Go!" each player picks up an egg by sucking in on the straw and carries the egg to his or her small dish. Whoever picks up the most eggs wins the game!

Playful Bunnies

There are 8 bunnies hiding in this picture. Can you find them? *(Answer on page 24)*

Which Two Chicks Are Alike?

(*Answer on page 24*)

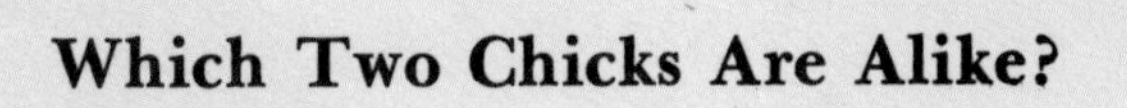

Watching Things Grow

To make lima beans (or peas) sprout, dampen a few sheets of paper towel and lay them on a tray. Put the beans on top. Cover the tray with clear plastic wrap.

Lift the plastic wrap and add a little water each day. In a week or so, you will see a root and then a sprout growing from each bean!

To make carrots sprout, stick two toothpicks into the top of a carrot and put it in a jar of water. Soon roots will appear on the bottom and green shoots will grow from the top!

Make Your Own Jewelry

To make a dandelion chain, cut a slit through the stem of a dandelion. (Ask a grownup to help you.) Then slide a second dandelion stem through the slit. Make a slit in the second stem and add another dandelion. Keep on going until your flower chain is as long as you want it. The chain can be a belt, a wreath for your hair, or even a collar for your dog!

Noodle jewelry is fun too. Just paint straight macaroni noodles with poster paint. Thread a big needle with strong thread. String the noodles, and then tie the ends of the thread together when your necklace is the size you want.

FOLLOW
ARROW ON
NEW ROAD
GO AHEAD
3
FOLLOW
ARROW TO
GRANDMA'S
MOVE AHEAD
3
GO
BACK TO
START
FORGOT TO
LOCK
DOOR
STOP
TURN RIGHT AT
STOP SIGN
TAKE
SHORT CUT
START

A Spring Drive to Grandma's House

This is a board game for two or more players. Use a different kind of coin or button for each player's piece. To find out how many spaces to move, throw one die. Players take turns moving along the road. The first player to reach Grandma's house wins!

Make a Rabbit

To make this rabbit, you will need an empty spool of thread, a clothespin, glue, poster paint, and felt-tipped pens.

Glue the clothespin on top of the spool. Then paint the whole thing white or pink. When the paint is dry, draw eyes, nose, and mouth with pens. You can dress up your rabbit with yarn, buttons, sequins, or anything you want!

Make a Duck

This adorable duck is made of two pom-pons. To make the body, first cut a strip of cardboard 8 inches long and 1¼ inches wide. Tape a piece of yellow yarn to each end. Then loosely wind the yarn from your spool around the cardboard until it is as thick as a small drinking glass (you will wind the yarn about 180 times). Take the tape off the cardboard and tie the single string of yarn very tightly. Slip out the cardboard. Now cut through the rounded yarn and fluff your pom-pon!

To make the head, do the same thing but wind the yarn only half as many times.

Attach the two pom-pons by running a pipe cleaner through the centers and bending the ends. Cut out cardboard feet, bill, and eyes using the patterns below. Fold the bill in half. Paste the bill and the eyes on. Now you can play with your duck—or put him in your Easter basket!

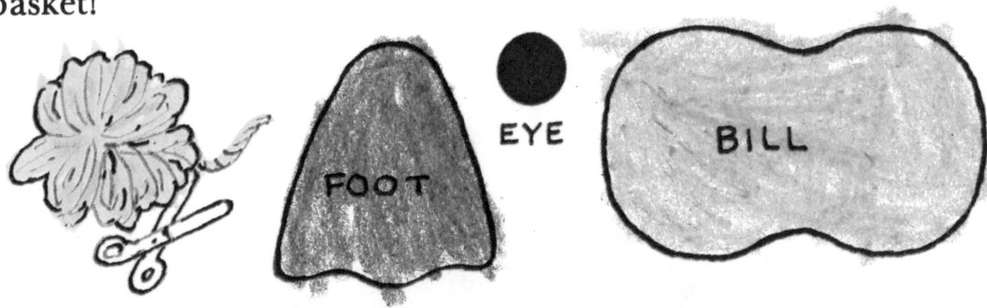

A Treat for the EASTER BUNNY

When the came up on Easter morning, the hopped into the garden with a full of . He hid the for the children between the . Then the found a bunch of that the children had left for him. What a nice surprise!

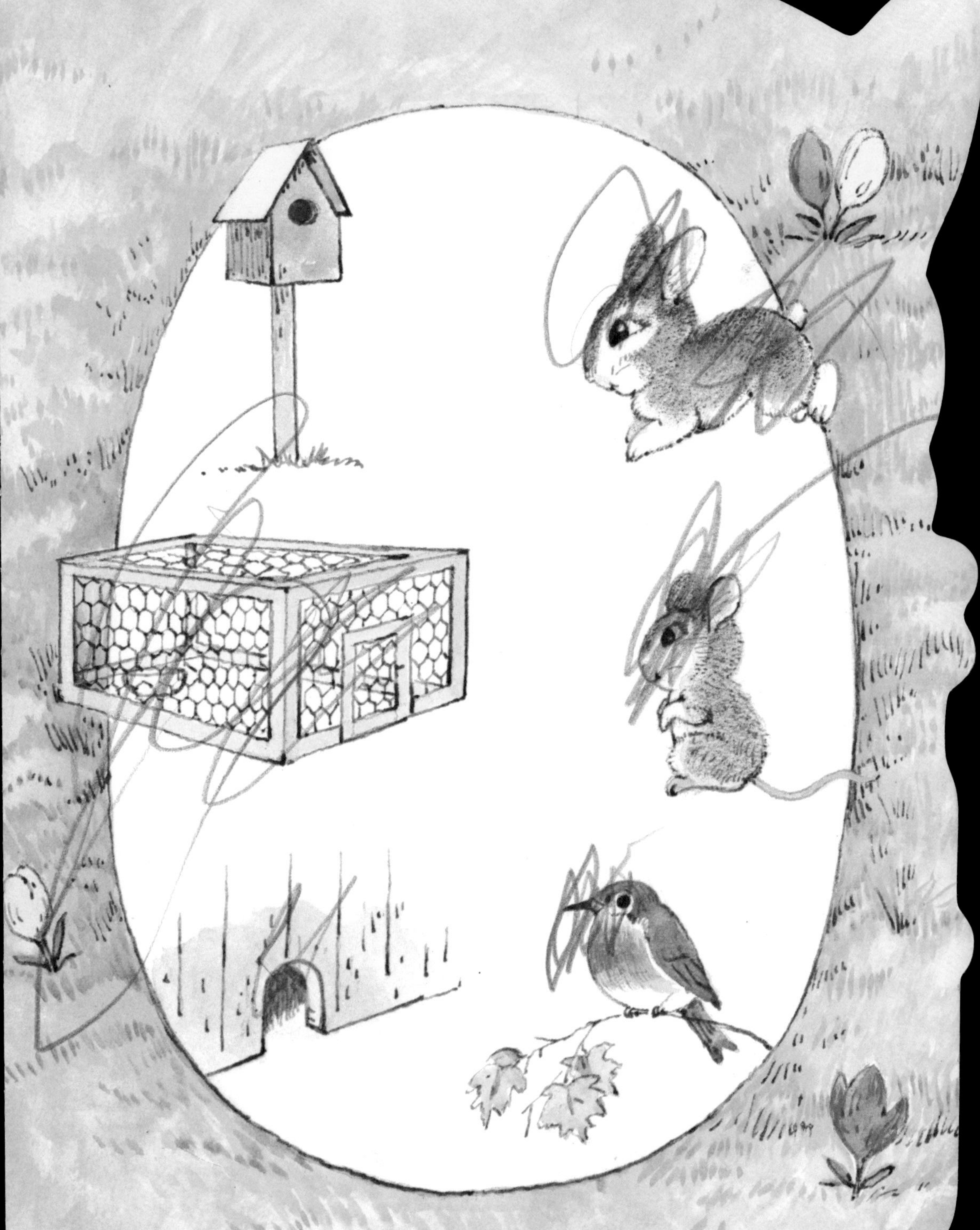

Animals at Home

Which animal lives in which house? *(Answer on page 24)*

Make Egg Animals

To make egg animals, you will need a blown-out egg for each. To blow out an egg, poke a hole at the top and bottom, using a large sewing needle or a small knitting needle. (Ask a grownup to help you.) Make the bottom hole slightly larger than the top. Hold the egg over a dish and blow through the top hole until the eggshell is empty.

Paint each eggshell with light-colored poster paint. When the paint is dry, add eyes, nose, and mouth. For holders, cut four strips of paper, each measuring 1¾ inches long and ½ inch wide. Tape the ends together to make four ring-shaped holders.

To make ears, chicken comb, and beak, trace the shapes below onto thin paper. Color them and cut them out. Then fold the bottom parts along the dotted lines in the patterns and glue flaps onto eggs. Pipe cleaners or broom straws can be glued on for whiskers. You will have the cutest cat, rabbit, chicken, and mouse ever!

TRACE
THIS
PATTERN
FOR
EGGS

Make an Easter Egg Tree

To make your own Easter egg tree, first find a few bare branches. Fill a coffee can with dirt or stones and push the branches into the can. (You can also decorate the outside of the can with pretty wrapping paper.)

To make the Easter eggs and leaves, trace the patterns on pages 18 and 19 onto thin paper as many times as you want. Color and cut out your eggs and leaves. Then fold them in half and hang them on the branches. What a pretty Easter decoration!

Make Paper Flowers

To make these lovely spring flowers, practice drawing circles and ovals by tracing the ones on this page. Then copy them onto colorful construction paper. (To make violet petals, cut circles in half.) Then, just overlap your paper petals using paste, and paste pipe cleaners onto the backs of your flowers for stems. Put them in a jar and you have flowers that will last and last!

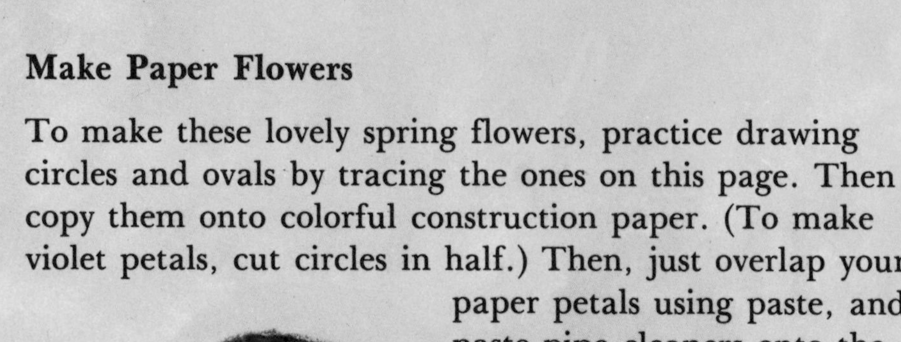

Easy Animals to Draw

You can draw all the animals on this page using only circles, squares, rectangles, and ovals! Which animal do you like best?

Egg Hunt

Can you find the 6 Easter eggs hidden in this picture?
(Answer on page 24)

Who Is Watching the Easter Bunny?

To find out, just connect the dots.

Answers

A-mazing Bunny *(page 2)*

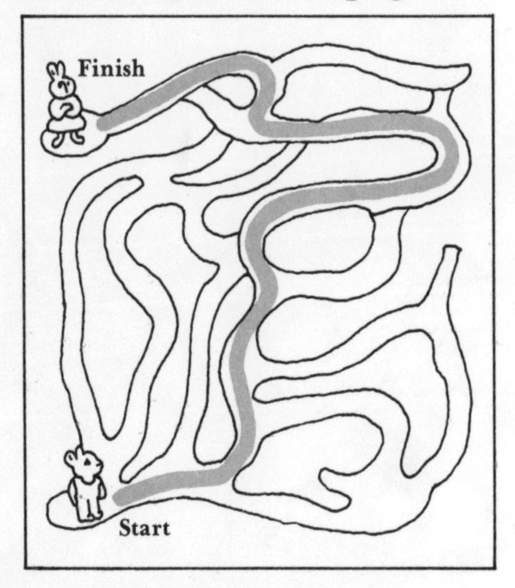

Which Two Mice Are Alike? *(page 3)*
The two mice wearing red raincoats with no pockets.

Playful Bunnies *(page 6)*

Which Two Chicks Are Alike? *(page 7)*
The two chicks with feathers on their hats.

Animals at Home *(page 15)*
The bunny lives in the cage. The mouse lives inside the hole in the wall. The bird lives in the birdhouse.

Egg Hunt *(page 22)*